ALL-TIME FUNNIEST

JOKES

ABOUT DINOSAURS

Little Mitchie
an imprint of Mitchell Lane

Creating Young Nonfiction Readers

Little Mitchie **lets children delve into nonfiction at young reading levels. Young readers are introduced to new concepts, facts, ideas, and vocabulary.**

Tips for Reading Nonfiction with Young Readers

Talk about Nonfiction

Begin by explaining that nonfiction books give us information that is true. The book will be organized around a specific topic or idea, and we may learn new facts through reading.

Look at the Parts

Most nonfiction books have helpful features. Our *Little Mitchie* titles include color photographs and graphic aids, a table of contents, a glossary, and an index. Share the purpose of these features with your reader.

Color Photos and Graphic Aids

A lot of information can be found by "reading" photos, charts, maps, and other graphic aids found within nonfiction texts. Help your reader learn more about the different ways information can be displayed.

Table of Contents

Located at the front of the book, this list shows the big ideas within the text and the page numbers where they can be found.

Glossary

Located at the back of the book, the glossary defines key words and phrases that are related to the topic. These words and phrases can be found in the text in colored type.

Index

Located at the back of the book, an index is an alphabetical list of topics and the page numbers where they can be found.

With a little help and guidance about reading nonfiction, you can feel good about introducing a young reader to the world of *Little Mitchie* nonfiction books.

Mitchell Lane
PUBLISHERS

2001 SW 31st Avenue
Hallandale, FL 33009
www.mitchelllanepub.com

Little Mitchie

First Edition, 2025.

Author: Kim Thompson
Designer: Kathy Walsh
Editor: Luana Mitten

Names/credits: Kim Thompson
Title: All-Time Funniest Jokes
About Dinosaurs / Compiled by Kim Thompson
Description: Hallandale, FL:
Mitchell Lane Publishers, [2025]

Series: All-Time Funniest Jokes
Library bound ISBN: 979-8-89260-263-1
Paperback ISBN: 979-8-89260-422-2
eBook ISBN: 979-8-89260-272-3

Little Mitchie is an imprint of
Mitchell Lane Publishers

PHOTO CREDITS
Adobe Stock: GraphicsRF, 6, 8, 9; YG Studio, 10; Alamy: SARAWUT PADUNGKWAN, cover, 1; Rosanne Tackaberry, 10; Stocktrek Images, Inc., 12; Elena Malgina, 13; Felix Choo, 15; leonello calvetti, 15; Chronicle, 20; Mohamad Haghani, 20; Shutterstock: V_ctoria, cover, 1, 22-23; Phai, 4, 10, 14, 16, 18, 20; Ken Benner, 4; I'L YELLOW, 4; YarynaBo, 5; armancatalasan, 5; Puwadol Jaturawutthichai, 6; Giuseppe_R, 6; CitraDesignPro, 7; Eatvector, 8; Mountain Brothers, 9; clushy, 9; Anatolir, 9; HitToon, 11; Shutterstock AI, 11; 75ChuanStudios, 12; Sudowoodo, 13; klyaksun, 14; Ain Mikail, 14; Sarah Freder, 16; Teras_Universe, 16; Victor Brave, 16; Cory Thoman, 17; Black-Pearl, 17; Gorodenkoff, 18; Shamanska Kate, 18; Marques, 19; Buch and Bee, 19; Sarunyu L, 21; klyaksun, 21

CONTENTS

DINO-MITE!

Q: WHERE DO DINOSAURS GO ON VACATION?
A: TO THE DINO-SHORE!
Q: WHAT DOES A DINOSAUR GET FOR MAKING A TOUCHDOWN?
A: A DINO-SCORE!

Q: WHERE DO DINOSAURS SHOP?
A: AT THE DINO-STORE!
Q: WHAT KIND OF DINOSAUR LOVES HARRY POTTER?
A: A DINO-SORCERER!

T. REX

Q: WHAT SHOULD YOU DO IF YOU SEE A T. REX?

A: HOPE THAT IT DOESN'T SEE YOU!

Q: WHAT DO YOU CALL A T. REX'S TEMPER TANTRUM?

A: A FIT FOR A KING!

WHAT DO YOU CALL A T. REX THAT...

Q: WEARS A COWBOY HAT?
A: *T. TEX!*

Q: CRASHES ITS CAR?
A: *T. WRECK!*

Q: DOES YOGA?
A: *T. FLEX!*

Q: WEARS GLASSES?
A: *T. SPECS!*

Q: BROKE UP WITH ITS GIRLFRIEND?
A: *T. EX!*

TRICERATOPS

Q: WHAT HAS THREE HORNS AND FOUR WHEELS?

A: A TRICERATOPS ON A SKATEBOARD!

Q: WHERE DOES A TRICERATOPS SIT DOWN?

A: ON ITS TRICERA-BOTTOM!

Q: WHICH DINOSAURS MAKE THE BEST POLICE OFFICERS?

A: TRICERA-COPS!

Q: WHAT IS THE NAME OF THE DINOSAUR'S T-SHIRT SHOP?

A: TRY SARAH'S TOPS!

STEGOSAURUS

Q: WHY IS THE STEGOSAURUS SUCH A GOOD VOLLEYBALL PLAYER?

A: BECAUSE IT CAN REALLY SPIKE THE BALL!

Q: WHAT DINOSAUR LEFT ITS ARMOR OUT IN THE RAIN?

A: A STEGOSAUR-RUST!

Q: WHY IS THE STEGOSAURUS POPULAR AT DINNER PARTIES?

A: BECAUSE IT BRINGS ITS OWN PLATES!

Q: WHAT DO YOU CALL A SLEEPING STEGOSAURUS?

A: A STEGO-SNORE-US!

PTEROSAURS

Q: WHAT DO YOU CALL TWIN PTEROSAURS?
A: PAIR-ODACTYLS!
Q: WHAT DO YOU CALL A PTEROSAUR DRESSED UP FOR HALLOWEEN?
BOO!
A: A SCARE-ODACTYL!

Q: WHY IS A PTEROSAUR SO QUIET IN THE BATHROOM?
A: BECAUSE ITS "P" IS SILENT!
Q: WHEN DID PTEROSAURS ATTEMPT TO FLY?
A: DURING THE TRY-ASSIC PERIOD!

MORE DINOS

Q: WHAT DOES AN ANKYLOSAURUS SAY BEFORE SWINGING ITS TAIL AT A PREDATOR?
A: "WELCOME TO THE CLUB!"
Q: WHY IS A BRACHIOSAURUS SLOW TO APOLOGIZE?
A: BECAUSE IT TAKES A LONG TIME TO SWALLOW ITS PRIDE!

Q: WHAT DOES A ***HADROSAUR*** SAY AT THE END OF A MEAL?

A: "PUT IT ON MY BILL!"

Q: WHY DOES THE ***ARCHAEOPTERYX*** CATCH THE WORM?

A: BECAUSE IT IS AN EARLY BIRD!

WHAT-O-SAURUS?

Q: WHAT DINOSAUR IS INVISIBLE?
A: THE NEVER-SAUR-US!
Q: WHAT DINOSAUR SEES ALL?
A: THE SPY-NOSAURUS!

DINO DIGS

Q: DO PALEONTOLOGISTS ENJOY THEIR WORK?
A: YES, THEY DIG IT!
Q: HOW CAN YOU TELL IF A DINOSAUR HAD GOOD DENTAL HYGIENE?
A: FROM ITS FLOSS-ILS!

Q: WHERE DO YOU FIND THE FOSSILS OF LAZY DINOSAURS?
A: IN SEDENTARY ROCKS!
Q: WHAT DO YOU CALL THE BONES OF THE LARGEST DINOSAURS?
A: COLOSSAL FOSSILS!

PREHISTORIC TIMES

Q: WHICH TOURIST ATTRACTION CLONED ONLY LONG-NECKED DINOSAURS?

A: GIRAFFE-IC PARK!

Q: WHY DIDN'T THE DINOSAUR CROSS THE ROAD?

A: BECAUSE THERE WERE NO ROADS BACK THEN!

MORE LAUGHS

What did the T. Rex say to Woody after he ate a toy? *"You've got a friend in me!"*

Which reindeer do dinosaurs dislike? *Comet!*

What happens when there is not a real dinosaur in your house? *A fossil-arm!*

Why are dinosaurs the life of the party? *Because they are tons of fun!*

Why don't dinosaur skeletons attack museum visitors? *Because they have no guts!*

Why shouldn't you take a dinosaur bone on a train? *It will jostle your fossil!*

HOW TO TELL A JOKE

1. Relax. If you feel awkward, your audience will too.

2. Don't rush. Give your joke some space and trust that it's a good one!

3. Vary your tone. Your voice should not be flat or boring.

4. Pause right before the punchline. This will add some drama!

5. End right on the punchline. Don't keep talking or try to explain.

6. If you don't get a laugh, that's okay. Try another joke!

GLOSSARY

"I GET IT NOW!"

Ankylosaurus (ANG-kuh-loh-saw-ruhs): a type of dinosaur that had a bony club at the end of its tail

Archaeopteryx (AR-key-ahp-tuh-riks): a prehistoric bird that was about the size of a crow and had reptile-like characteristics such as teeth and a long bony tail

Brachiosaurus (BRA-kee-uh-saw-ruhs): a huge type of dinosaur that had longer front legs than hind legs

hadrosaur (HAH-druh-sor): a bipedal dinosaur that had a crest on its skull and a snout shaped like a duck's bill

paleontologists (pay-lee-uhn-TAH-luh-jists): scientists who study fossils and ancient life-forms, including dinosaurs

pterosaurs (TAIR-uh-sors): members of a group of extinct flying reptiles that includes pterodactyls

INDEX

FURTHER READING

Cheeky Monkey. *Hilarious Jokes*, Puns, Riddles & Pranks: *A Tickle-Your-Funny-Bone Book for Silly Kids Who Love to LOL*. Atglen, PA: Better Day Books, 2024.

Katz, Alan. *The Funniest Joke Book Ever for Kids!* New York: Scholastic, 2024.

Riddleland. *The Jumbo Book of Funny Jokes for Kids*. Prospect Park, PA: BCBM Holdings, 2023.

ON THE INTERNET

Good Housekeeping: 125 Knock Knock Jokes for Kids and Adults Who Love to Laugh https://www.goodhousekeeping.com/life/parenting/g36198919/knock-knock-jokes-for-kids/ Silly jokes to fool your family members and friends!

Parents: 100 Jokes for Kids That Will Actually Make You Laugh https://www.parents.com/fun/entertainment/14-jokes-for-kids-that-will-actually-make-you-laugh/ A source for Dad jokes, one-liners, puns, and more.

Today: 150 Funny Jokes That Will Get the Family Laughing https://www.today.com/parents/family/jokes-for-kids-rcna49138hat/Find jokes about seasons, animals, and more.

ABOUT THE JOKESTER

Kim Thompson is a teacher, writer, and editor. Things that make her laugh out loud include going down waterslides while holding her feet in the air, trying to balance a grape on her nose, and the dopey expressions that turtles get on their faces. She lives with her husband and two funny cats in Columbus, Ohio.